HOW BIG IS OUTER SPACE?

By Rebecca Storm

CONTENTS

First published in 2026 by Hungry Tomato Ltd
F15, Old Bakery Studios, Blewetts Wharf, Malpas Road,
Truro, Cornwall, TR1 1QH, UK.

Thanks to our editor, Julie Tofflemire.

ISBN 9781835694374
Manufactured in the USA

Discover more at
www.hungrytomato.com

All words in **BOLD** can be found in the glossary.

WHAT CAN YOU SEE WHEN YOU LOOK AT THE NIGHT SKY?

You might see a big shining object called the Moon. You might see lots of little bright lights called **stars**. You can even see some larger bright objects called **planets**. You can see some planets with your eyes. But you'll need a **telescope** to see them in detail.

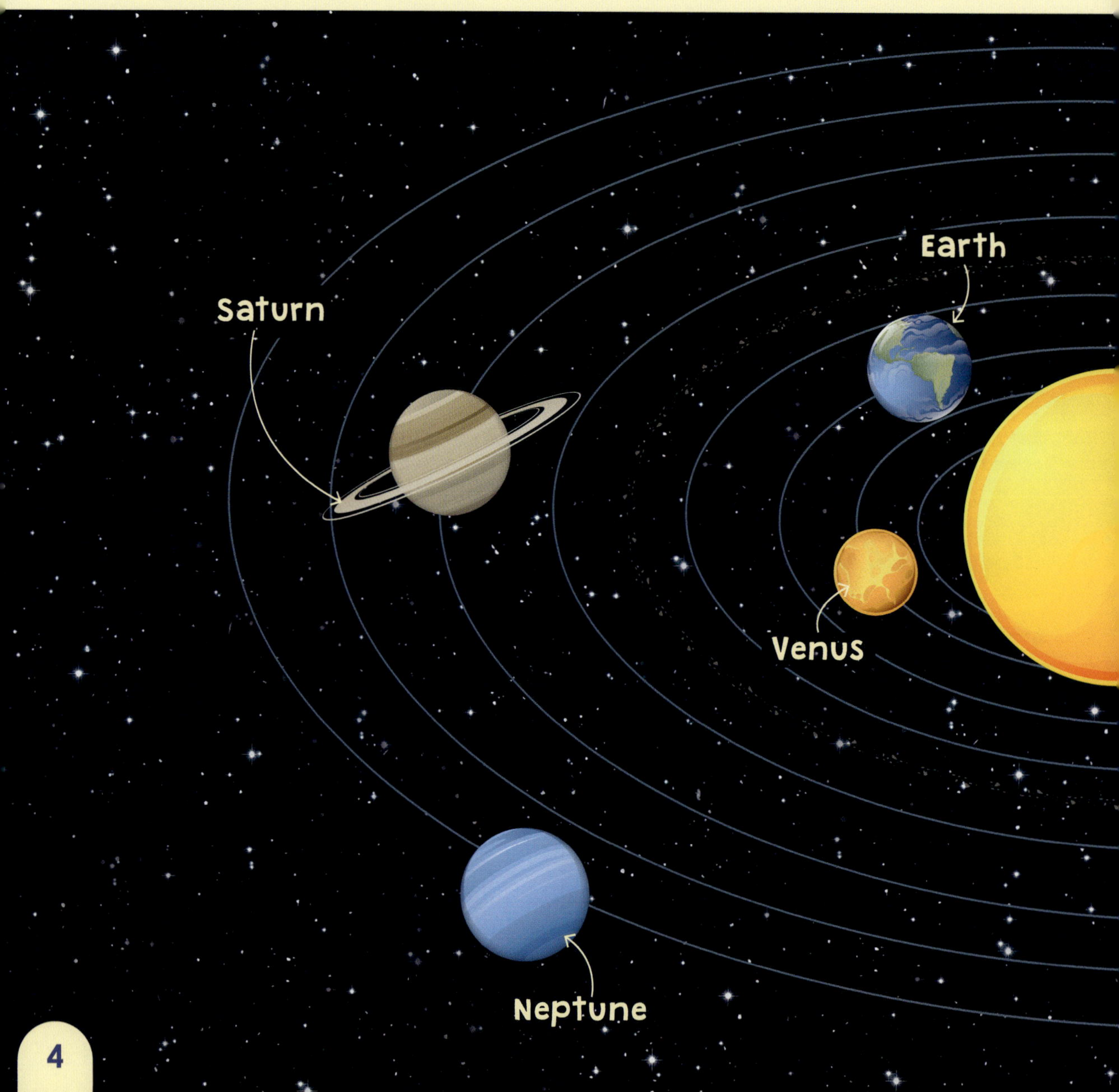

Planets, moons, and one star called the Sun make up the **solar system**.

All the planets go around (**orbit**) the Sun.

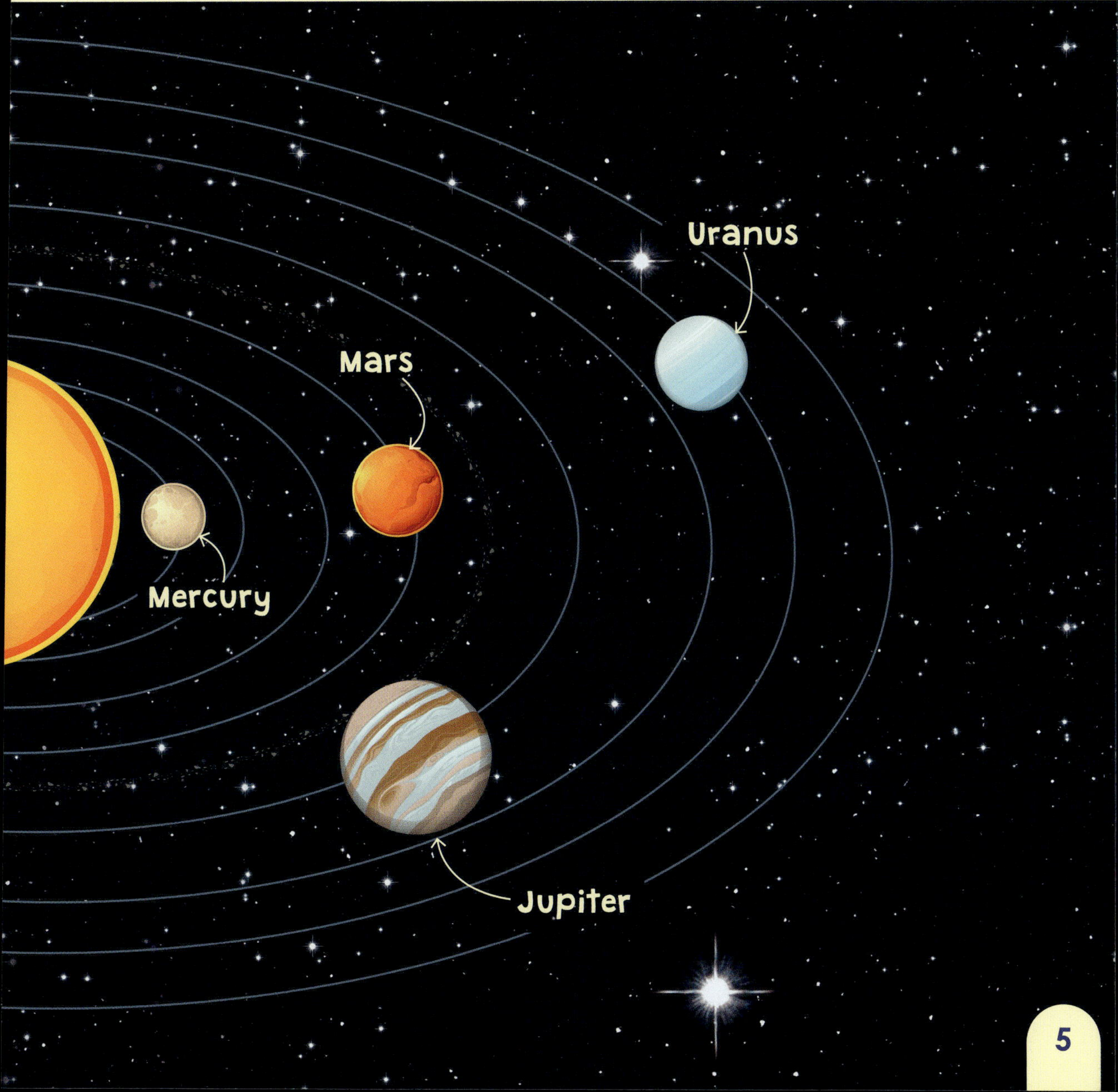

WHY IS THE SUN SO IMPORTANT?

The Sun is a small star.

Most stars make heat and light by turning **hydrogen gas** into **helium gas**.

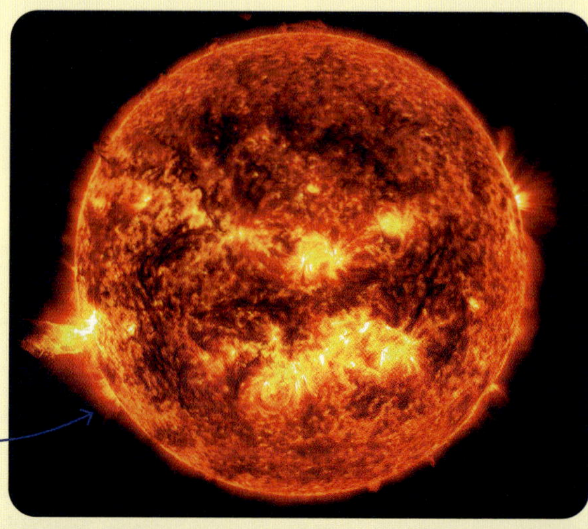

THE SUN'S IMPORTANCE

Without the Sun, our planet would always be dark and freezing cold. We would not be able to live here.

The Sun gives the warmth that makes living things grow.

Our body creates vitamin D from the Sun, which keeps us healthy.

The Sun is a long way from us, but its heat is so powerful that it can burn our skin, unless we protect ourselves with sunscreen.

HOW LONG WOULD IT TAKE TO WALK TO THE SUN? Answer on page 23!

The Sun is the center of the solar system. All the other planets orbit around it.

REMEMBER
You must never look directly at the Sun. It can damage your eyes!

WHICH PLANETS ARE NEAREST TO THE SUN?

Mercury is the nearest planet to the Sun. It's also the smallest planet in our solar system.

Mercury

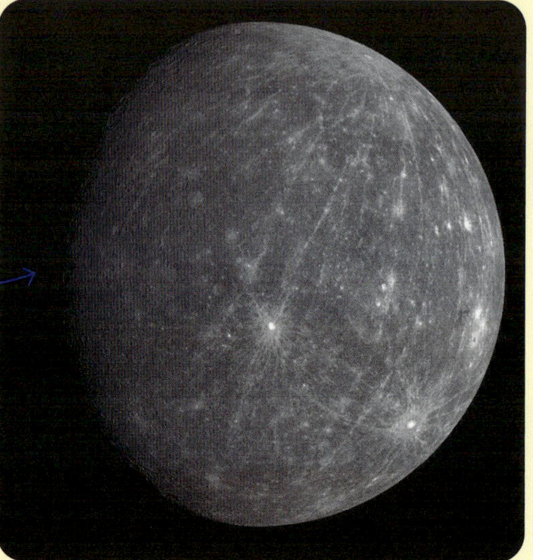

MELTING METAL!

It is so hot on Mercury that metal would melt on its **surface**.

Venus is the second planet from the Sun. It is the hottest planet because its thick clouds traps in the Sun's heat.

Venus has an **atmosphere** so **poisonous** that nothing can live there.

It is the planet that is closest in size to Earth.

HOW TO SPOT VENUS

Through a telescope, you can see Venus in even more detail.

If you look in the morning, you can see Venus rising before the Sun comes up.

Venus

WHICH PLANET IS A GOOD PLACE TO LIVE?

Earth is a good place to live. It is neither too hot nor too cold. Earth is our home.

It is the only planet that we know of where people, animals, and plants can live.

Earth

SUPPORTING LIFE

A lot of Earth's surface is covered with water. All living things need water to drink.

Earth's air also has enough **oxygen** for us to breathe.

Some places on Earth are very hot, like deserts.

Some are very cold, like the ice sheets of Antarctica.

Ice Sheets

Desert

ALL SHAPES AND SIZES!

Earth is just right for all types of life. From the very tiny...

... to the **very large!**

WHY IS EARTH SUCH A GOOD PLACE TO LIVE? Answer on page 23!

WHY DOES THE MOON CHANGE SHAPE?

The Moon is always orbiting Earth.

It takes about one month for the Moon to make one trip around Earth.

The Moon

THE PHASES OF THE MOON

Half of the Moon is lit by the Sun and half is in **shadow**. Different amounts of the Moon's face are lit up depending on where the Moon is in its orbit. This is why the Moon appears to change shape.

We know a lot about the Moon because it has been visited by **space probes** and by **astronauts** in **spacecraft**.

MAN ON THE MOON

The Moon has no water, no weather, and no air.

When astronauts visited the Moon, they had to wear special **spacesuits** to help them breathe.

WHAT MAKES THE MOON SHINE?

Answer on page 23!

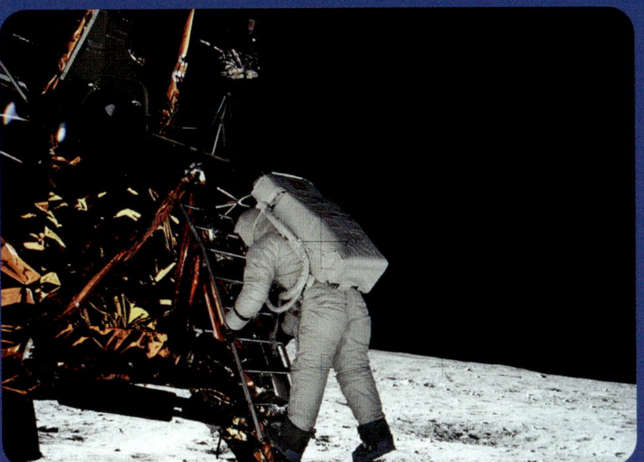

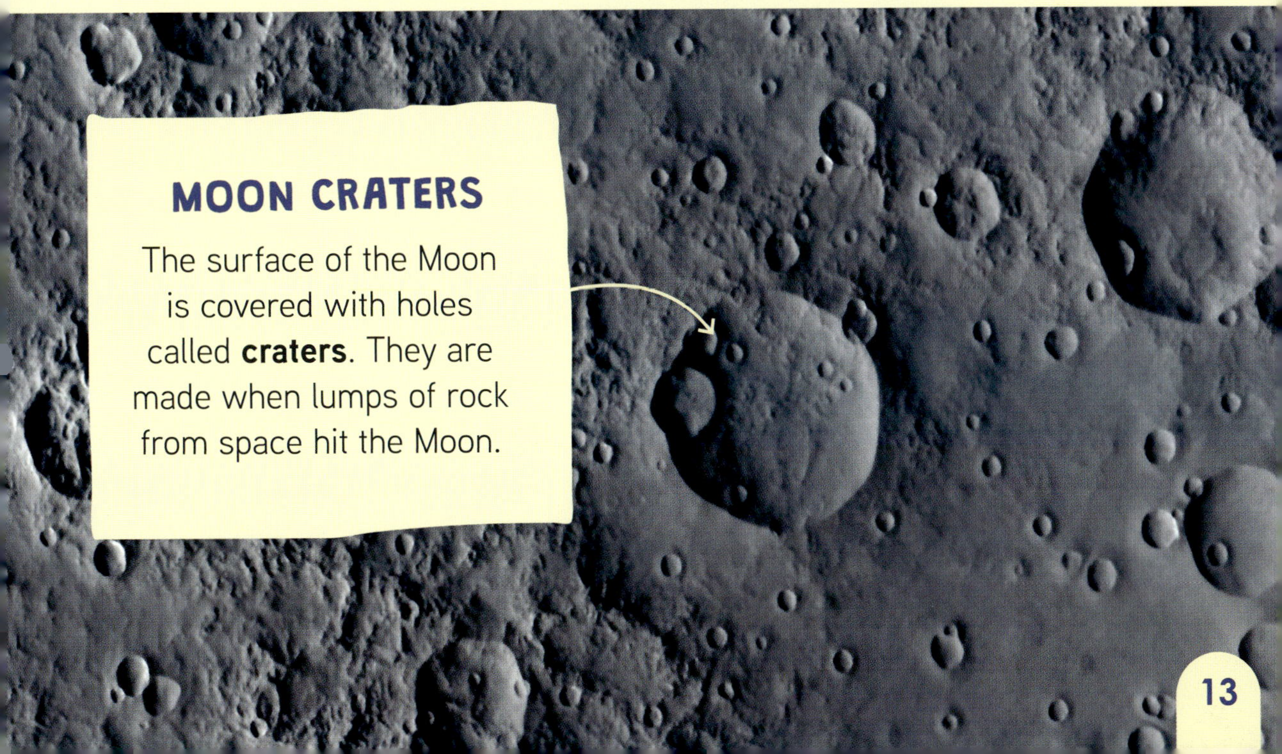

MOON CRATERS

The surface of the Moon is covered with holes called **craters**. They are made when lumps of rock from space hit the Moon.

WHY IS MARS CALLED THE RED PLANET?

When you see Mars through a telescope, it looks quite red.

This is not because it is hot but because it has very red soil.

Mars

Mars is smaller than Earth. But it has two moons and the biggest volcano in the solar system.

VISITING MARS

No astronaut has ever gone to Mars, but there are robotic machines sent by scientists that have landed on the planet.

Landers and **rovers** are robotic machines scientists have sent to Mars to learn more about it.

Scientists know there is frozen water on Mars.

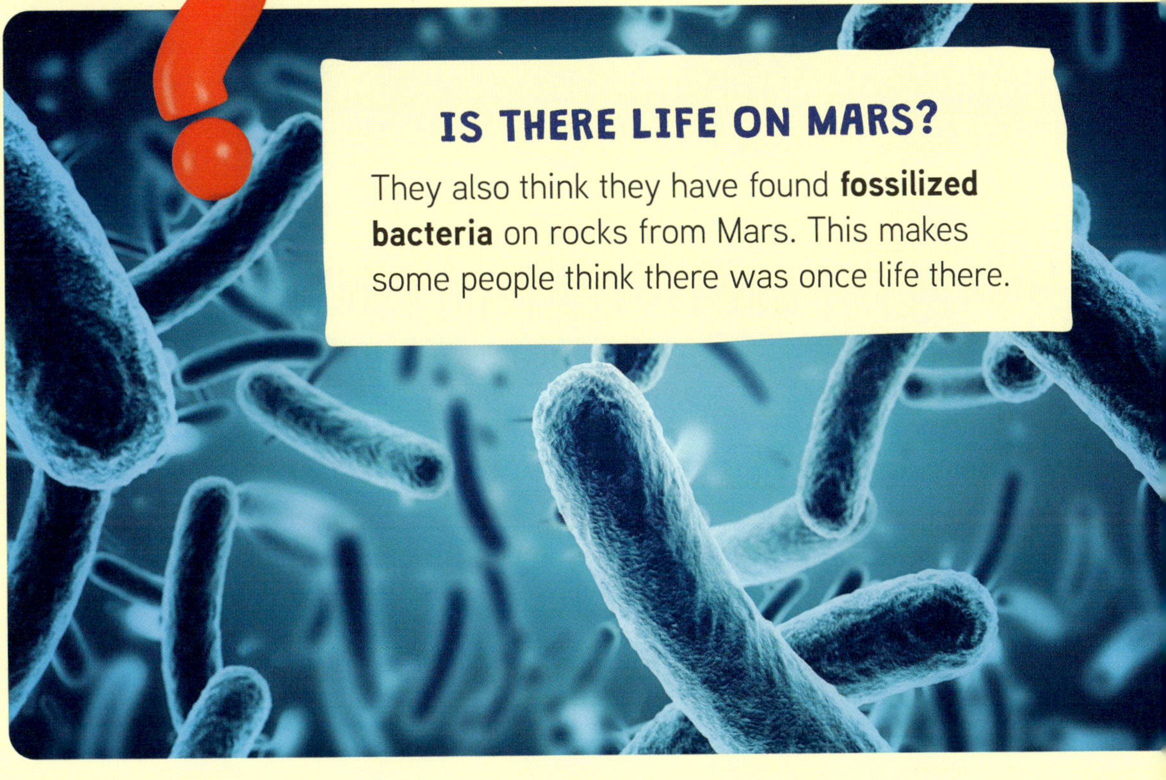

IS THERE LIFE ON MARS?

They also think they have found **fossilized bacteria** on rocks from Mars. This makes some people think there was once life there.

DO YOU THINK WE COULD LIVE ON MARS?
Answer on page 23!

WHICH PLANETS ARE THE BIGGEST?

The solar system has two giant planets. They are Jupiter and Saturn.

They both shine brightly and are easy to spot, even without a telescope.

Jupiter

Saturn

SATURN'S RINGS

Saturn is famous for its rings. They are made of lots of pieces of rock, dust, and ice.

Jupiter is the biggest planet in the solar system.

It is more than twice as large as all the other planets put together.

JUPITER'S BIG STORM

Through a powerful telescope, you can see that Jupiter is surrounded by bands of **gas**.

Jupiter also has a huge red spot. This is actually a massive storm that has been blowing for years.

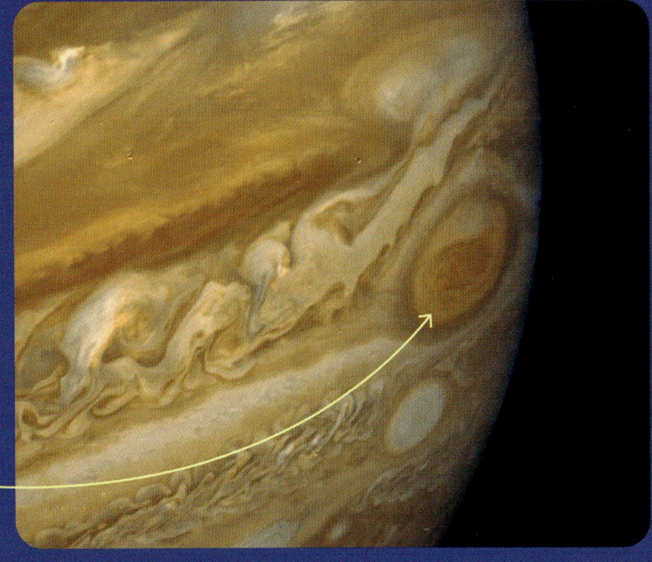

HOW MANY RINGS DOES SATURN HAVE?
Answer on page 23!

WHICH PLANETS ARE FARTHEST AWAY FROM THE SUN?

Uranus

Neptune

FREEZING COLD!

Uranus and Neptune are far, far away from the Sun. Because they are so far away, the Sun's light is too weak to warm them up much.

They are icy planets, colder than the coldest place on Earth.

Space probes have flown past Neptune and Uranus to find out more about the planets.

These planets are very stormy places. A storm spot just like the one on Jupiter has been seen on Neptune.

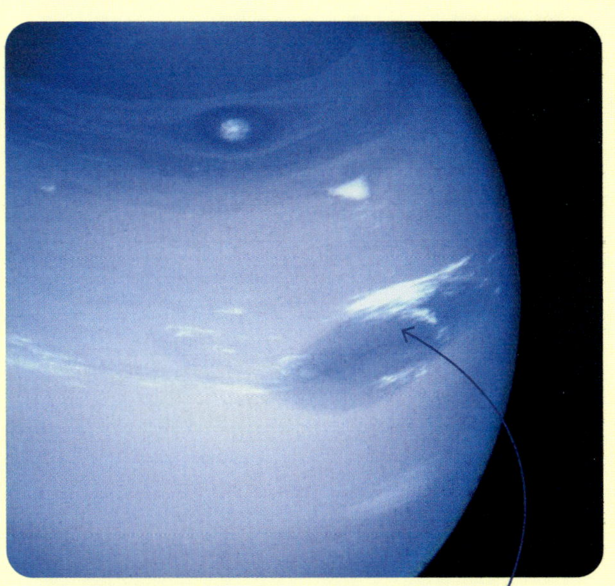

Neptune's storm spot

WHAT IS THE KUIPER BELT?

Beyond Neptune's orbit, you can find the **Kuiper Belt**. Its shape is a thick disc, like a donut.

The Kuiper Belt is full of millions of objects, including **dwarf planets**, like Pluto.

Pluto

WHAT DO YOU THINK WOULD HAPPEN IF YOU LANDED ON PLUTO? Answer on page 23!

HOW BIG IS OUTER SPACE?

Outer space is huge! Deep space is everything in the **universe** beyond Earth.

This includes not just the planets, but small pieces of loose rock inside the solar system. When these rocks fall to Earth, they are called **meteorites**.

Meteorite

PREPARING FOR IMPACT!

Sometimes much bigger rocks called **asteroids** crash into Earth. This huge crater was made by an asteroid around 50,000 years ago.

Scientists use special equipment to investigate deep space.

In 2021, **NASA** launched the James Webb Space Telescope.
It can see far out into space.

WHAT'S OUTSIDE THE SOLAR SYSTEM?

Our solar system is just a tiny part of a **galaxy** called the Milky Way.

There are many other galaxies, too.

James Webb Space Telescope

Scientists have also sent probes to gather information about objects in space.

EXPLORING THE UNIVERSE

We may never explore the whole universe. It keeps getting bigger, so there would always be new parts of it that remain undiscovered!

Image captured by James Webb Space Telescope

WHAT DOES IT TAKE TO BE AN ASTRONAUT?

Answer on page 23!

In case they meet other forms of life, some space probes carry information about Earth.

GLOSSARY

Asteroids - large rocks in space that are the size of small planets.

Astronauts - people who travel in space.

Atmosphere - the air that surrounds a planet.

Craters - holes in a surface made by rocks hitting it, or by volcanoes.

Dwarf planets - nearly round objects that orbit the Sun, but are not large enough to clear their orbits of smaller objects.

Fossilized bacteria - the remains of tiny organisms (living things) that lived in an earlier time and became enclosed in rock.

Galaxy - a huge grouping of stars.

Gas - when some things are heated, they turn into a gas. Water turns into a gas called steam. The air we breathe is made of many gases.

Helium gas - a colorless gas with no smell. The Sun makes its energy by changing hydrogen into helium.

Hydrogen gas - a light gas that burns easily. The Sun turns hydrogen into helium to make energy.

Kuiper belt - a large area beyond Neptune where small, icy objects can be found.

Landers - spacecraft that land on other objects in space, such as a planet or moon.

Meteorites - chunks of rock from space that have fallen to Earth.

NASA - the National Aeronautics and Space Administration is an organization in the USA. It sends spacecraft into space to study our solar system and beyond.

Orbit - when an object moves around something in a set path.

Oxygen - a part of the air needed by people and animals to breathe.

Planets - balls of rock or gas that orbit the Sun.

Poisonous - dangerous to eat, drink, or breathe.

Rovers - robotic vehicles that can move around and collect information on planets and space objects.

Shadow - a dark area created by the blocking of light.

Solar system - the name for the Sun and the planets and moons that go around it.

Space probes - spacecraft without people on them that explore space.

Spacecraft - a machine made to travel in space.

Spacesuits - clothes the astronauts wear to protect them in space.

Stars - large balls of burning gas, far away in space.

Surface - the outside part of a planet or moon, or the top part of something, like the sea.

Telescope - something we look through. It makes things seem closer and more detailed.

Universe - everything in space, including Earth, the solar system, and galaxies.

Could you answer all the questions? Here are the answers:

Page 7: It would take over 3,000 years for a person walking nonstop to get to the Sun!

Page 8: Not a good idea! Mercury's atmosphere is so poisonous that nothing can live there.

Page 11: Earth has air we can breathe, water we can drink, and it is the perfect temperature for life.

Page 13: Light from the Sun bounces off the Moon and makes it look bright in the sky.

Page 15: Not yet, but some scientists think that we may be able to build a base on Mars and live there in the future.

Page 17: Saturn has seven ring groups made up of thousands of rings.

Page 19: It is so cold on Pluto that your body would freeze in under a minute!

Page 21: You need to study hard, especially in science and math, be physically fit, and be good at teamwork to become an astronaut.

INDEX

Picture credits:
(t=top; b=bottom; m=middle; l=left; r=right):
Shutterstock: Ade Triansyah73 1bg, 20bl; Alfmaler 4-5bg, 9tr; Artsiom P 14tr, 14b, 15tr; Claudio Caridi 16b, 16mr, 19mr; Dawid Sawila 6b; Den Rozhnovsky 12br; Dima Zel 21tr; Eric Isselee 11bl; Florian Nimsdorf 14ml; G_hang.out 7 (icon); GoodFocused 11br; GTW 11tl; HelenField 13b; Igoran_vector_3D_render 15 (icon); Jacopo Minetta 17t; Ljupco Smokovski 9br; Lukasz pawet Szczepansk 7b; Mario Savoia 20b; Maxim Ibragimov 7tr; Myroslava Bazhko 10b; NASA images 18ml, 18mr; Pavlista 15m; Pe3s 16ml; Remigiusz Gora 8b; Sabbir Digital 11tr; Sanit Fuangnakhon 20ml; SmartS 12ml; Smit 18b. Nasa: images-assets.nasa.gov/image/GSFC_20171208_Archive_e001435/GSFC_20171208_Archive_e001435~orig.jpg 6tr; images-assets.nasa.gov/image/PIA11245/PIA11245~orig.jpg 8tr; images-assets.nasa.gov/image/PIA00104/PIA00104~orig.jpg 9bl; images-assets.nasa.gov/image/GSFC_20171208_Archive_e002131/GSFC_20171208_Archive_e002131~orig.jpg 10tr; images-assets.nasa.gov/image/GSFC_20171208_Archive_e000868/GSFC_20171208_Archive_e000868~orig.jpg 12tr; images-assets.nasa.gov/image/as11-40-5868/as11-40-5868~orig.jpg 13tr; images-assets.nasa.gov/image/PIA01370/PIA01370~orig.jpg 17mr; images-assets.nasa.gov/image/PIA19708/PIA19708~orig.jpg 19br; https://images.nasa.gov/details/PIA01142 19br; images-assets.nasa.gov/image/GSFC_20171208_Archive_e002063/GSFC_20171208_Archive_e002063~orig.jpg 20tr.

Every effort has been made to trace the copyright holders, and we apologize in advance for any unintentional omissions. We would be pleased to insert the appropriate acknowledgments in any subsequent edition of this publication.